I0429001

NATION BUILDING: VOLUME III
FOUNDATIONAL DOCUMENTS

By:

Mark Carven Olds, MNO, CNM, CPE

NATION BUILDING: VOLUME III

By:

Mark Carven Olds, MNO, CNM, CPE

The success of this volume shall interlace in the fact and existence of its purposeful incompleteness. This very unusual success barometer shall point to the requirement of additional minds to relay their expertise to form a "Collective Genius."

Unity will only be achieved among the among the imperfect people and the impoverished people after a process has been set forth that can attract persons, who have the courage and willingness to go the distance to make a difference. The amalgamation shall occur as skilled laborers, progressive individuals, and justice seekers will assist in the implementation of plans and theoretical concepts. Models must give way to the practice of committed action. Unity shall emerge through non-traditional and non-historical strategies....

NATION BUILDING: VOLUME III
FOUNDATIONAL DOCUMENTS

Mark Carven Olds, MNO, CNM, CPE

Copyrights 2016

NATION BUILDING: VOLUME III

FOUNDATIONAL DOCUMENTS

BY

MARK CARVEN OLDS, MNO, CNM, CPE

THE *"FOUNDATIONAL DOCUMENTS"* WILL PRESENT WRITTEN ENCAPSULATION READY FOR DISSEMINATION THAT SHALL RELEASE STRUCTURED INFORMATION. From these instruments, individuals can access the principles and precepts of Nation Building. The candor and delineation shall represent the courageousness to provide truth of position without qualms or reservations. Ambiguity having been removed, the information can be studied, analyzed, and critiqued for its substance alone. The format shall also permit the adopted views to be prayerfully read and spiritually discerned.

Support of the Immanuel Nation In Christ (INIC), as distinguished and identified by such documentation, shall open the door for both challengers and champions. Challengers can state their opposition that may be based upon the incompleteness of the premise. Champions shall view the documents as a syllogism to a positive presupposition to build a nation. Champions shall respond to the cause with commitment and fervor, while challengers will look for ways to lament and infuse doubt. Support of the INIC must be aggressive, not passive. Nationhood will call for people, who have vision. The pathway of Nation Building will not be for everyone, only those who will dare to believe that God shall always stay a Covenant-Keeping God.

DEDICATION

To the beloved memory of

Willie Grey Olds

And

Ida Mae Wilkes Olds

NATION BUILDING: VOLUME III

FOUNDATIONAL DOCUMENTS

Table of Contents

FOUNDATIONAL DOCUMENTS

Preface:

This volume shall present an intentional incomplete work. The mission of this document will be to broaden and enlighten the populace and observers to the basic tenets that shall be required in nationhood. It shall describe the task of preparation in reference to the essentials that must be executed. Rarely will undertaking achieve the desired outcome in an unfulfilled assignment. The break with traditional paths of procedure will be clearly illustrated. Rather than present a model that will not include all that shall be coveted, this work in progress shall extend an invitation to the masses a well as individuals to conjugate with the exertion. Being candid at this juncture, an invitation will be extended for others to become a part of the initiative. The volition should reach an evangelistic thrust in nature to inform people that they must act now.

The success of this volume will interlace in the fact and existence of its purposeful incompleteness. The very unusual success barometer shall point to the requirement of additional minds to relay their expertise to form a "Collective Genius."

Unity will only be achieved among the among the imperfect people and the impoverished people after a process has been set forth that can attract persons, who have the courage and willingness to go the distance to make a difference. The amalgamation shall occur as skilled laborers, progressive individuals, and justice seekers will assist in the implementation of plans and theoretical concepts. Models must give way to the practice of committed action. Unity shall emerge through non-traditional and non-historical strategies.

A commitment ethos has to be employed. An inundation of positive and obtainable change has to become an internal beckon. The fusion will illuminate the pathway to Nation Building. Challenges will summon a greater resolve to move forward to nationhood.

The foundation basis of the Immanuel Nation In Christ (INIC) shall consistently rest upon the Word of God. The Lord has declared His love for justice.[1] The world and its fullness always has and always will belong to Him.[2] His Sovereignty shall preclude whatever has currently come into existence as human declared boundaries or limits. The principle component of the INIC will reveal faith. Faith without works will be pronounced dead.[3] Nation Building shall validate the works of faith, having been made alive for the imperfect people and the impoverished people.

The INIC shall be supported by these two principles: God has set the boundaries of men,[4] the government shall rest upon His shoulders,[5] and He shall supply all our needs according to His riches in glory.[6] In addition, He has declared Himself God, Who can make, keep, and operate by covenant. He has covenanted with Abraham to make him the father of many nations.[7] God shall keep a covenant unto a thousand generations.[8] He has retained the authority and the power to raise up a nation in one day.[9] Nothing has ever been too hard for Him.[10] Incontestably, nationhood, as brought forth through the INIC shall fit within these guiding principles.

The *Foundation Documents* will present a written dissemination that shall release structured information. From these instruments, individuals will access the principles and precepts of Nation Building. The candor and delineation shall represent the courageousness to provide truth of position without qualms or reservations. Ambiguity having been removed, the information can be studied, analyzed, and critiqued for its substance alone. The format shall also permit the adopted views to be prayerfully read and spiritually discerned.

Support of the Immanuel Nation In Christ (INIC), as distinguished and identified by such documentation, shall open the door for both challengers and champions. Challengers can state their opposition that may be based upon the incompleteness of the premise. Champions shall view the documents as a syllogism to a positive presupposition to build a nation. Champions shall respond to the cause with commitment and fervor, while challengers will look for ways to lament and infuse doubt. Support of the INIC must be aggressive, not passive. Nationhood will call for people, who have vision. The pathway of Nation Building will not be for everyone, only those who will dare to believe that God shall always stay a Covenant-Keeping God.

Notes:

[1]Isaiah 61:8 NASB

[2]Psalm 24:1 KJV

[3]James 2:17 and 20 KJV

[4]Acts 17:26 KJV and NASB

[5]Isaiah 9:6 KJV

[6]Philippians 4:19 NASB

[7]Genesis 17:4-5 NASB

[8]Deuteronomy 7:9 KJV

[9]Isiah 9:6 KJV

[10]Jeremiah 32:17 KJV

Introduction:

As a result of the covenant by God, Abraham had become the father of many nations. Nothing can be located in the Scriptures would suggest the end of nations coming into existence. A nation dispensation doctrine cannot be proclaimed. God has not set in place a restriction or limitation on the era that nations that were to be attributed to Abraham's fatherhood would appear. The 21st Century has not suddenly become too distant or too far removed from the promise to Abraham by God that He (the Almighty) cannot deliver. This contemporary age cannot offer such sophistication that God's promises shall be nullified. Nation Building, by faith in the promises of God, has the power to spring forth, administering justice[1] on behalf of the imperfect people and the impoverished people. Nothing will ever be too hard for the Lord.[2]

Nations have continued to emerge in the natural. The majority of these nations (birthed in the 20th and 21st Centuries) have not acknowledged God, nor have they verbalized an acceptance of Jesus Christ. Conceivably, these sovereign states have not in any wise viewed their rise to nationhood as anyway related to the Abrahamic covenant. A nation, arising through faith, cannot be limited by the intellect of humanity.

Nationhood, as will be established in the Immanuel Nation In Christ (INIC), can only be a valid undertaking, if it has been properly aligned with the Holy Scriptures. Alignment with the Word of God shall provide an unstoppable force.[3] A nation, which has been built upon revelation[4] from the Word of God, shall move forward, undefeated. The imperfect people and the impoverished people, who shall seek an opportunity for fresh start- spiritually and naturally, must egress the current religious system and world system. The INIC shall provide the fresh[5] climate and fertile surrounding to foster nationhood.

The *Foundational Documents* shall enlighten and deliver to the populace (for the first time) a choice of status as delineated in Nation Building. The INIC will offer citizenship in a society without classism. This nation will not separate people into categories based on economic potential, political affiliation, or social pedigree. Within the INIC, equity and justice will not be mere terms of endearment, but sincere practice for all. The INIC shall strive to create an atmosphere for people to move forward. The INIC will not allow them to incessantly mull over the past and all of the shortcomings that can be attached failed efforts. The time has arrived to move the people forward. Offenses and attacks against this populace or personal imperfections may be eradicated in order that progress can be achieved. A classless, past-less society shall place the onerous squarely on each citizen to walk by faith and not by sight.[6]

The practice of Nation Building shall challenge every emotional, mental, physical, and spiritual fiber connecting the least prosperous to the current system. This concept's exertion will direct the populace away from the bondage and allegiance to status quo. The hold (a slave mentality) can paralyze through the fear factor. This fear factor can hold the populace into a habitual acceptance of a state of poverty or class limitation. Remaining in a hopeless state, the imperfect people and the impoverished people will no longer be able to cling to the absence of options excuse language. Such a position will no longer have merit. The INIC shall forever banish the ongoing excuse for doing nothing and preserving the status quo platform.

The INIC shall present a vantage that has not only arisen fresh, but very doable. Nation Building has become an interjection clearly within grasp. Nation Building shall exceed the realm of theoretical abstract thinking, but will function as a carefully crafted strategy. A strategic plan that can solicit participants, who will directly benefit from personal and direct engagement, shall form a systemic approach that may redefine holistic ministry and total service engagement.

As presented, the INIC will appear as a unique interpolation. It will not be a political comet, flashing on the dialogue pad of dialectic chatter. Nation Building will not fade as a social aberration, but will endure as a wholesome endeavor. This endeavor has been projected toward those who have grown weary awaiting political change, waiting on others to change, and generally waiting for things to get better. Applied action shall reward the active participants. Change shall occur by an individual's choices and decisions.

Notes:

[1]Isaiah 54:14-16 NIV

[2]Jeremiah 32:27 KJV

[3]Matthew 18:18 KJV

[4]Matthew 16:18 KJV

[5]Mark 2:21-22 AMPLIFIED

[6]2 Corinthians 5:7 NASB

Credo of Faith:

I shall not dare to be so presumptuous as to set forth a Statement of Faith for the Immanuel Nation In Christ in such a manner to even slightly offer a dogma as if all others that have come before or may currently exist me have been totally in error. I have become too fearful in my reverence of God Almighty, the Father of the Lord Jesus Christ, to even contemplate putting pen to paper as though I had absolute clarity of interpretation of all aspects of His Word. I certainly have not given Him counsel. This one thing that I have known, it can be a fearful thing to fall into the hands of the Living God, for our God has stated that a part of His nature will be reflected as a consuming fire. In taking the vision of the Immanuel Nation In Christ (INIC) from concept (heart) to implementation (reality), I have no wish to fall prey to a Pharisaic mentality, producing a founder's document to emerge into tradition, nullifying what has already been written.

With the aforesaid prologue, I shall speak what I believe will serve as a pillar, a beginning of my faith specific to this contemporary period. My maturation in faith will continue to direct me to always be open to hear the voice of the Holy Spirit. I have become unafraid to acknowledge that my theology may change, but I shall remain very much afraid to act obediently.

As an aspiring leader, I cannot hide behind a Statement of Faith that will be reflected in the INIC and not be willing to divulge what has arisen as my personal thoughts. Because I shall continue to grow in grace, a current stance may give way to a clearer revelation. The

Lord shall give wisdom from His will come knowledge and understanding. God has proven to be the only One who will not change. It would be easier for me to admit my shortcoming or frailty than to try and re-position a nation. Pride will precede a stumbling.

With all that shall surround the INIC, it shall be imperative that will walk by faith ant by any human system endorsement. I shall present a stable doctrinal position. In making a public declaration, I shall ascribe, "follow me as I follow Christ." I shall prayerfully ask the Father, "to search me and know my heart and see if there is any hurtful thing in me." I can be changed, questioned, and observed.

My Credo of Faith:

I.   I believe the Holy Scriptures is the inspired and infallible Word of God that was penned by holy men, who were moved by the Holy Spirit. I further believe that His Word is forever settled in heaven.

II.   I believe in the virgin birth of Jesus Christ, His deity, His subsequent death, burial, resurrection, and ascension.

III.   I believe in the Holy Spirit's presence inside the Born-Again Believer, residing as a Pledge, Comforter, Helper, and Teacher.

IV.   I believe that He will bodily return for the Believers, the Church.

V.   I believe eternal life commences with the acceptance of Jesus Christ as Lord and Savior and that nothing can separate me from the love of Christ.

VI.   I believe the Father is omnipotent, omnipresent, and omniscient.

VII.   I believe that hell (designed for the fallen angels) has enlarged itself and will be cast into the lake of fire where all non-believers in Jesus will spend eternity.

VIII.   I believe that there is no other way to come to the Father except through Jesus Christ, and there is no other name given among men whereby we must be saved.

IX.   I believe in the finished work of Jesus on the Cross of Calvary, whereby it is by grace that men are saved, not by works, and without the shedding of blood there is no remission of sin.

X.   I believe in water baptism by full submersion in the name of the Father, the Son, and the Holy Spirit; and that the celebration of the Lord's Supper, the Holy Communion are ordinances set forth in the Church by Jesus Christ.

XI.   I believe marriage is between one man and one woman.

XII.   I believe in pro-life with no exceptions permitting an abortion.

INIC: Example and Instruction

The Immanuel Nation In Christ (INIC) will form a paragon worthy of acceptance and approval. The INIC shall not seek to nullify the accomplishments of the successful. It will seek to elevate those who have been caught in the quagmire of despair. Those, who have been fortunate enough to have avoided or escaped the precarious entrapping predicament along life's journey, will not be the premier target populace of the INIC. The swelling pockets of poverty and expanding rolls of the forgotten, who have been entangled in the web of despondency, will have a safety net in the INIC. Covenant living will provide another start for multitudes to engage in productive and harmonious co-existence. Those, who the current system has rejected, will have a haven to repair their lives.

The light that shall illumine from the INIC will expose systems (political or religious) that must be avoided. With its appearance, other social systems must be compared beyond rhetorical put-downs. Humiliating remarks will never offer solutions. The model, which shall prove to be unforgiving and relentless in efforts to exclude the less than perfect, should be eschewed and evaded. A paragon, which will be open and welcoming, shall debunk the closed and rebuffing example.

Nation Building shall also present the INIC as the exemplar in the development of humanity. Those lives, which have been broken under the weight of a conundrum of forlornness, shall be able to find a resuscitation within the framework of the INIC. A representative sample from those who have been excluded from the profits, progress, and prominence of the current system, shall find equality, justice, and the means to contribute in the advancement of nationhood.

The INIC shall build upon a firm foundation that will be anchored in the Word of God. The Word has to come alive, not simply remaining ink on fancy parchment paper. Practices, which will denounce revival of the oppressed, will exclude the redemptive revelation of the Word. "For whatever was written in earlier times was written for our instruction, so that through perseverance and the encouragement of the Scriptures we might have hope."[1] The INIC will manifest the embodiment of the teachings of the Scriptures. These instructions will take a form to serve as a vessel that can perform a rescue of those who may have submitted to hopelessness. Reaching out to a vast number of hurting souls, Nation Building shall require steadfastness of purpose. In times of difficulty, the source of revitalization must arise from the Word of God.

The demonic forces (principalities and powers) will never express joy when aid has arisen for the oppressed people. Voices shall certainly surface in an exertion to vilify the noble efforts of reviving those who have been trapped in despair.[2] Such opposition will mandate a more concerted effort on behalf of those without a voice.[3] The task at hand will demand strength and the ability to convey helpful information. "For whatever was thus written in former days was written for our instruction, that by [our steadfast and patient] endurance and the encouragement [drawn] from the Scriptures we might hold fast to and cherish hope."[4] Building on the instructions from the Father, Nation Builders must hold a focus view, while patiently evangelizing and educating the populace. The Word shall function as a tool of encouragement to construct a composite whole for a people who have never had the opportunity to govern themselves. Resilience must have a formal introduction as a means to obtainment. Passion for positive achievement has to become freshly illuminated.

Black slaves in America were able to obtain hope through a process that could not have been visualized or even understood by the dominant culture, economic system, or societal order. Faith would enable the process that could keep a disenfranchised, abused people believing that justice was indeed inevitable, while assured that equality was a Divine impartation. God had retained His position of sovereignty and will forcefully defend the oppressed, the impoverished, those in bondage, the homeless, the fatherless, the foreigner, and all others who have a need of justice.[5] The abolition of the institution of slavery has not cleansed the ruling powers of all their iniquities. Much civility and practice of peaceful co-existence have resulted from the enactment of anti-equality laws. These anti-discrimination legislative laws have moved former slaves and former slave owners forward. The sophistication of classism has matched (in some instances overmatched) the dramatic legal implementations. The evolution of the level of equality in vogue today would not have arrived at this contemporary state by a single legislative maneuver. Countless lives were sacrificed in the fight for freedom with a humble attitude of victorious expectancy. The liberation struggle had been a fight for inclusion.

Classism had never bought into the inclusion argument and subsequently has never surrendered. Through carefully crafted manipulation of the culture definition, the economic system, and the societal norms, a large segment of the populace has remained excluded from the process of inclusionary practice. New enactments, with multiple collateral sanctions, has served as a disqualifying factor to keep numerous individuals from partaking of the gains that have been established by legalized enfranchisement. However, the current plight has been shared by multiple races. Nation Building will extend an invitation to all who have been codified and labeled inferior by an arbitrary and clandestine move of classism. This invitation shall ring loud to exit this current system and enter into a classless society.

The INIC will make an appeal to all (regardless of ethnicity). The appeal will beckon individuals to restoration in order to embrace a quality life in spite of imperfections. The problems than many within the multitudes have to face daily will find resolution in the INIC. Nation Building shall present the answer through the application of inclusivity in an orderly rule, nationhood.

Prayerfully, the INIC shall reach out to all who have the need of restoration and renewal. Many may lack the support network to facilitate a recovery from tragic mistakes or the consequences of misjudgments. The knowledge of God's Word can right the life ship for many of the downtrodden within the targeted populace. Not knowing the benefits of a right relationship with the Father will most often result from indoctrination into religion. The enlightenment that can be derived from the Word of God will serve as instruction throughout all ages. His Word shall always reign eternal. The collective volume of the Word of God shall always provide instruction. "These things happened to them as examples and were written down as warnings for us, on whom the fulfillment of the ages have come."[6] The INIC shall follow the examples of obedience, which will result in the blessings from the Lord.

Nation Building shall proffer a stratagem of escape from materialism, idolatry, and quiet assimilation of oppression. This practical implementation will make a way for the populace to embark on a journey toward stability and prosperity. Those, who have the least to contribute under the current system, will have the opportunity to reach their full potential both spiritually and naturally.

The INIC shall specify lessons and precepts, a way to live the revealed concepts. The populace will no longer only have enticing words from eloquent orators, but concrete action steps that can change their fate. Nation Building will position an individual to work toward an accomplished existence, rather than retaining a marred role as a statistic in a rubric.

Nationhood shall gain the attention of the populace. Nation Building will give needed directions. The INIC shall also deliver access to action strategies that can lead to the practice of solutions. Faith will enact the key to the emergence of the INIC.[7] Abraham, the friend of God, had received the promise of becoming the father of many nations by faith. The promise had not been made with a constraint to a geographical region, nor was the promise in any wise limited to a specific time period. The fatherhood of nations was never restricted in any capacity by the definition that may ascribe, nor the power that men may assess. The Divine authority can call into being what prelates cannot. Trusting exclusively in the Word of God, the INIC shall rest upon faith, the substance of things hoped for, the evidence of things not seen.[8] The promise to Abraham, the father of many nations, will still have the power of fruitfulness and productiveness in this contemporary age.

Notes:

[1]Romans 14:4 NASB

[2]Nehemiah 4:1-3 NIV

[3]Proverbs 31:8-9 NASB

[4]Romans 15:4 AMPLIFIED

[5]Psalm 146:7-9 KJV

[6]I Corinthians 10:11-12 NIV

[7]Romans 4:13-18 AMPLIFIED

[8]Hebrews 11:1 KJV

INIC Agenda:

The Immanuel Nation In Christ has a myriad of endeavors to include as future improvisations for the citizenship, who will embrace this initiative. The Immanuel Nation In Christ (INIC) has the following agenda:

> Evangelism[1]
> Education[2]
> Enactment[3]

A more specific litany of directions shall come into view with the input, the counsel, and the power and energy of the imperfect people and the impoverished people. Such an agenda cannot surface fully demonstrative without the advisory capacity of the skilled laborers, progressive individuals, and justice seekers. A nationhood agenda cannot come forward set in a vacuum, nor by a paternalistic few. A classless society must not duplicate the ways of a system that has fostered exclusion. A classless society will only thrive by inclusion of all the populace in determining how best to serve the multitudes.

Survey instruments must be disseminated through venues of beauty salons, barber shops, laundry mats, housing projects, community centers, community stores, door-to-door campaigns, street encounter campaigns, and wherever people gather formally and informally shall become an oasis of data accruement to help formulate the nationhood agenda. Perhaps, an even more effective methodology of information dissemination shall rest in direct communication with the people, word of mouth conveyance. Every individual must feel in their soul that have been heard and respected. After information has been assembled, it will become assimilated into a strategy to implement solutions to an item that has been slated for the INIC agenda. An agenda, without follow-up solutions or verifiable action steps toward resolve, would simply evolve as another example of a rhetorical exercise of futility. A response of this nature would have all the earmarks of an action plan, but would actually operate as a conduit for extensive dialogue. The imperfect people and the impoverished people should not function as another source or topic for additional people discussing their issues. These discussion usually will come minus any substantial steps of reform or a process toward problem solving.

The INIC Agenda shall list the items with a solution to address the area of concern. If the concern merits listing, then the listing merits a solution. Nation Building has arisen as agenda, not an activities list. A laundry list of problems without solutions will only chart a course set to continue the overall conundrum.

Notes:

[1]Nation Building: Volume I
The Portrait of a Movement
(The Transition to Nation Building)

[2]Nation Building: Volume I
The Portrait of a Movement
(The Transition to Nation Building)

[3]Nation Building: Volume I
The Portrait of a Movement
(The Transition to Nation Building)

INIC Manifesto:

The Immanuel Nation In Christ (INIC) will make public its declaration and intention for the populace. Nation Building will produce a classless society, which shall permit those who have been excluded from full participation in the existing system a means of re-connecting to societal achievements. Through the exertion of the INIC, covenant living shall assure each individual the opportunity to realize a quality life existence possibility.

The current system will disqualify an imperfect person from re-entry into the system in a meaningful participatory capacity above a minimal level. Nation Building shall make a way for the imperfect people to cease participating in the caste system. Nation Building shall offer a way of dignity revitalization. The INIC will not have any camouflaged exclusionary clauses.

The exigency of the INIC will result from people desiring change and embracing the vehicle than can deliver. Transporting obscure lives onto a stage, the INIC will embody a vehicle than can reflect the full potential of humanity. This may be accomplished through faith toward God. The people, who will affix themselves to the INIC, shall view Nation Building as achievable in their lifetime. Nation Building will uphold life, enhance life, and preserve life.

The purpose of the INIC will act to raise the consciousness of the imperfect people, the impoverished people, the skilled laborers, the progressive individuals, and the justice seekers to the level of nationhood. The imperfect people and the impoverished people shall also receive the resolution and the determination to cherish Nation Building.

The skilled laborers, progressive individuals, and justice seekers must find the theoretical, spiritual, and intellectual mix to invoke Nation Building. The INIC's message should tout an outreach to all humanity with the purpose of improving their quality of existence.

There should exist an urgency to rescue or deliver from danger a segment of the general populace. This should detonate multiple methods to relay the message of Nation Building. The INIC will assure the imperfect people and the impoverished people that God's blessings, readily available, shall make for a future and a hope. Legacy building shall commence with victories over the current blight of injustice, poverty, imprisonment, oppression, depression, and economic instability. Nation Building shall represent an opportunity to create an inheritance, develop a positive legacy for a generation whose lives have been twisted by imageries of darkness. The INIC shall extend a place for the displaced, a light to those who have been or currently have found themselves in darkness.

Divine essence will make imperative the aim of the INIC to eliminate second class citizenship by providing equality, respect, and accessible opportunity. The INIC will respect the laws of the land, but God's law shall reign supreme. During this contemporary age, this world system (dominant and economic forces) will habitually reinforce itself. As an integral part of its perpetuation and power to sustain its dominion, this world system will seek to control, eradicate, or remove any and all undesirable elements.

The firm foundation of Nation Building shall rest upon the Word of God, a covenant promise to Abraham that he would be the father of many nations. This promise to him was by faith. The dependency of the INIC shall unequivocally originate with God. Undeniably, Christ shall forever remain the corner stone. The multitudes in search of an expressive and meaningful life transformation must have been exposed to this Biblical truth. Advocates of Nation Building cannot retain an unrealistic envisage that persons with public influence will yield their forums to the INIC or become its ambassadors. The message has to spring passionately and fervently from the hearts of those embracing Nation Building. These individuals shall shoulder the responsibility of widely spreading the message. The disseminating of the teaching that will lead to nationhood has to become a witnessing tool, which can direct people into the family of God, the kingdom of God, and the INIC. Each individual should marshal the burden to share with a relative, a neighbor, a friend, a casual acquaintance, or someone recently encountered. There has to be an urgency brewing within the messenger's spirit in order to disseminate the message to any new or old, familiar or unfamiliar person.

An individual versed in the Doctrine of Nation Building should identify as a part of the formation of an "away team." To reach the variant audiences, innovative thought has to become interjected into the relevancy of the targeted audience. Each venue must have a design to engage the people with an expectation of maximum productivity. The creation of workshops, seminars, forums, colloquiums, focus groups, community learning sessions, home meetings, telephone marathons, chat rooms, e-mail, internet marketing, prayer meetings, prayer vigils, public gatherings, festivals, dialogues in parks, recreation centers, and other ideas to assemble people to present nationhood, Nation Building, and the INIC have to be exploited.

A new paradigm cannot unfold by retaining reliance and a dependent relationship with the old. A fresh motif cannot avoid a graded series of creative tension between the time honored and the contemporary. The INIC's consummation of action will mandate an egress from the existing world system.

Impelling the initiative, the INIC will not exhibit a clandestine approach, nor a stealth methodology. In spurring the populace into action, a premier step will command the overcoming procrastination and an indifferent posture, if not an abrasive attitude toward the implementation of nationhood. People must have their spirit stirred in order to move, to take a course of action. The core of leaders attached to Nation Building must have an authentic connection and an unalloyed relationship with the populace. The successful rise of the INIC will exact servant-leaders not in search of personal acclaim. These men and women shall possess an alacrity unique as a genre of leadership willing to lay down their lives for the least of their brothers and sisters. Such an attribute shall identify with covenant living. A commitment to the INIC will dictate a response to a calling to serve others. The privilege to serve others will reign as the priority; next, will come the recognition of the honor to represent those who will be served. The dedicated disciples of Nation Building shall attain stature as leaders of the INIC.

The INIC shall insist upon direct action. The lacing of dialogue with acrimonious attacks minus solutions shall only record empty and senseless fodder. Nation Building will extend far beyond a stimulating political debate. The INIC will always have a result oriented mission. Nationhood will far surpass an alternative theory for academicians to overstate or intellectuals to overemphasize in debates.

Philosophical contrasts cannot minimize or maximize the INIC. This endeavor will move the populace from concept to strategy, and finally to implementation. In this undertaking, immediate steps must occur. Passivity has no place on the agenda.

Through Nation Building, the INIC shall deliver its views. While the INIC will look intently at the concerns of the populace, the premise of nationhood will stay open to inspection. The INIC shall proffer solutions to the populace through the following:

SEEK HIS KINGDOM – Each citizen of the INIC must seek His kingdom. The INIC shall present itself as the epitome of achievement. The INIC will not obtain for its citizenry a pass into the presence of God, nor will it have the capability to acquire a preferential relationship status with Him. Jesus has already authorize the only authentic passage to the Father. Nation Building shall stress the doctrine of Jesus as the way, the truth, and the life. Ascertaining the knowledge of His kingdom will implore virtuous and honorable living. The craving to live in His kingdom will insist on the practice of righteousness. In the life of an individual or the practice of a nation, the preeminence of Christ shall assure a state of blessedness. Diligence in obedience to the Lord will set a nation above those who shall fail to heed righteousness. Furthermore, promotion shall come to the nation that will establish Christ first. Such a nation shall excel the surrounding nations who will not acknowledge the exalted preeminence of Christ. The INIC shall recognize this Biblical mandate. The INIC shall build on the foundation of Christ, seeking His kingdom and giving Him the preeminence. With such a firm foundation, ridicule and malignant assaults cannot cause to exist an interference vigorous enough to prohibit the favor of God.

COVENANT LIVING – A nation build upon covenant living shall exceed the cohesiveness of a republic. Covenant living has as a definition - a people coming together as one, sharing resources, seeking a collective success; Divinely inspired. Covenant living, as a pillar, can build and sustain a nation. Covenant living shall also possess the essence to transpose a small body of people into a nation. A covenant with God shall stand stronger than any democracy. A covenant relationship with the Father shall assure the INIC victory over all obstacles. Nation Building, through covenant living, shall knit the people together in the Spirit, in the bond of love, and the bond of peace; thereby, a classless society shall surface. Only covenant living can produce an interlacing act of people set on a firm course toward Nation Building. No legislative act or executive order can force people to live in harmony and continue bias free. A nation, practicing unconditional love for one another, will exist as a united people. Covenant living shall release communication with God in an uninterrupted flow. The favor of God shall reign paramount in Nation Building. His presence will remind the pioneers of the INIC that success shall rest in Him.

ONENESS AND UNITY – Oneness shall disclose that impeccable attainment can develop today. Unity can breathe in vision and will exhale success. Oneness will communicate a single purpose. Nation Building will not demand the historiography of similitudes of prior evolutions, when the foundational doctrine shall rest upon the preeminence of Christ. Nation Building, which shall image the aforementioned doctrine, will harmoniously guide the people to preferred results. Acting out of a single motive with one consequence in mind, Nation Building shall demonstrate oneness. Unity will not look critically for cracks in another's armor. Unity shall seal the leaks and will strengthen what was previous exposed as vulnerable. Unity will also broaden the prospective and shall narrow the chance of failure. Unity can pour out life as showers and may absorb shortcomings into a river of opportunity. Unity shall rejoice and will shout victory as the imperfect people and the impoverished people will then reach out to the skilled laborers, the progressive individuals, and the justice seekers. The vision of Nation Building and the INIC shall only realize an accomplished state through unity. Unity will not insist upon the majority of the populace, but only those who can exercise agreement among the committed.

APOSTOLIC ORDER – Within the INIC, the apostle shall hold the lead role of guiding the people spiritually and worshipfully. The worship aspect, as a foundational pillar of Nation Building, shall point emphatically to Christ. Twelve apostles were chosen by Jesus. Upon His Ascension, He was empowered to give spiritual gifts to men. The apostle was positioned to head this list. The traditions of associations, conferences, denominations, trends, and corporate influences have altered titles as well as functions. The order of government systems will not carry over into the INIC. The preponderant influence of the existing system will not find fertile ground in the INIC. The final evidence of hegemony shall be destroyed through Nation Building and the INIC. The cultural, ideological, social, and economic influences that have been exerted under the current system shall have no avenue of entrance into nationhood under the INIC. The foundation of Nation Building and the INIC will not succumb to the pressures of historical models.

THE REGIONAL CENTERS – The regional centers shall serve the dual purpose of fortified outpost and the launch pad of systemic deployment. The centers shall further act as cities of refuge. These zones of refuge shall provide restoration, relocation, and recovery. The regional centers shall serve as the palpable subsistence where lives may undergo transformation. People will be able to from doctrine and theory to implementation and practicality. The regional centers will give the INIC a physical presence. Nation Building shall move from the regional centers into the urban areas. A reciprocal flow shall occur. Live that have experienced negative effects in urban area may seek healing at one of the regional centers that may be located in a rural area, while lives that have experienced healing at one of the centers can return as a thriving witness to metropolis. Both will have become equipped to share the experience of a personal revelation of the Nation Building message. Through planning and training, the message and the vision has to get delivered in a systemic approach, which shall reflect Nation Building.

ECONOMIC ENGINES – The INIC will be sustained by internally crafted and created economic engines. These economic engines will conduct themselves as the revenue generators that will supply the financial stimulus that can move the forward dramatically the initiatives and programmatic processes. The INIC will develop a profitable Gross National Product (GNP). The INIC will remove the imperfect people and the impoverished people from the ranks of consumers only. Initially, goods and services will be produced within the INIC. Afterwards, these products shall become available to consumers outside the INIC. The INIC has no intention of ever being mistaken as an entitlement program. Nation Building shall rely upon the provisions of God and the skill set that has been invested in its citizenry. God Almighty will always teach His people to profit. He will give them witty inventions. He shall uncover for His people the hidden wealth. Hoarded treasures of darkness have been promised to His people. Nation Building shall exercise a systemic approach to building lives, recovering lives, and restoring lives through covenant living. More than enough resources have already been put into existence to make the INIC happen.

GOVERNANCE – The INIC will be sustained through a vigilantly structured governing system, which shall rely on covenant living as its base of operation. Governance shall implant, the direction, the control, and the administration of policy. The governance of the INIC will exist of the people and for the people with the Holy Spirit directing all outcomes. The INIC shall make obsolete a bureaucratic assembly of lawmakers (no legislative branch). Laws of men cannot restore life. No legislative branch could ever pass any semblance of a life giving statute. The imperfect people and the impoverished people shall receive a life giving flow from the Spirit, not another list of laws from men destined to be broken. Nation Building will point the way to an accessible wisdom to all who will cradle the INIC.

MINISTERS OF THE CABINET – In addition to spiritual gifting, each Minister of the Cabinet must have an area of expertise and the anointing to carry out the particular purpose. The INIC shall enact twelve cabinet posts. The cabinet shall oversee the functions that will guide the operation of the INIC. A relationship with God will always serve as the dominate prerequisite for any individual to ascend to the role of Minister of the Cabinet. The spiritual gifts must have been demonstrated, before a natural responsibility shall become assigned. Without the anointing of God, academic, intellect, and professional experience will only obtain a natural result. Nation Building will never settle for or focus on being average.

NATION BUILDING – Nation Building shall create an opportunistic vehicle for imperfect people to achieve success; whereas, the current system will impose upon the same population disqualifying sanctions. Nation Building will represent the formal teachings and activities that can lead to the structure and infrastructure conducive to a nation's emergence. The combination of teachings and activities will serve as the foundational instructions of the INIC. Nation Building will transcend the cultures and dogmas of others. Nation Building shall reach outside of mere passion or strong will. This endeavor shall work an intrinsic commitment that will function in spite of volatile elements or negative criticism. Nation Building will enlist more than an exercise in liberal conscious appeasement. Nationhood shall include the presupposition of expansion. The resolved aspiration of Nation Building will labor to raise the quality of life of the people through a classless society. The combination of existential factors shall make Nation Building practical and something to behold. It can be grasped as a concept, prayed over as a vision, and accomplished by unity.

ENTREPRENEURIAL   SOCIALISTIC ENGAGEMENT – Nation Building will institute the Entrepreneurial Socialistic Engagement as its economic system. This will employ an economic systems within Nation Building that shall oversee the commerce of the populace, while encouraging individual ownership in supplemental initiatives. For most people to grapple simultaneously with multiple challenges across numerous fronts would compose an unrealistic expectancy. Theocratic and socialistic enactments will battle the cultural, political, and religious, and social indoctrination of most people. Change that will exist as more than a feel good exercise shall only come with a high cost. This will ring especially true of economic change. Rhetoric has no room in a ministry that will challenge the methods that industries shall conduct business and consumers will engage in revised expenditure habits. This enormous effort will not seek to reform what has already been entrenched, but will set forth a new knowledge base outside of the existing system. The oppressed have always besought God for a plan of justice. The time has once again arrived. Issues that plague the populace will not go away, unless a substantial segment of the populace will embrace truth and shall become proactive in response to the revelation. The Entrepreneurial Socialistic Engagement shall deliver:

1. *An economic system that will be responsive to fellow human beings in the deployment of quality living conditions and future potential enhancement.*

2. *An economic system that will oversee the commerce of the populace, while encouraging individual ownership in supplemental initiatives.*

3. *An economic system that will promote inclusiveness in revenue generation and revenue sharing.*

4. *An economic system that will have its roots in covenant living.*

5. *An economic system that shall spawn and will support the social initiatives of a populist movement.*

6. *An economic system that will be dedicated to the interlocking of faith with works.*

7. *An economic system that will be principled to safeguard against exploitation, materialism, and narcissistic societal influence.*

The pathway of Nation Building will not find acceptance by everyone. This concept shall not reflect a statement of exclusivity based on a prejudicial bias. Only those, who will dare to believe that God will continue as a Covenant-Keeping God, can take this adventurous pilgrimage. Most antagonists will fear change. The pathway of Nation Building will present a road for travel not mere observation. It will require the mobilization both of people ideology. It will never exist as a stasis pathway, but an encyclical that shall point toward movement for beliefs and people. The pathway will not discover an exemption from a rough course. In fact, it may uncover an experience filled with demur and remonstrance. The passageway shall have illumination, which will reflect a method or mode that can change values, morals, doctrinal positions, and disciplines that may run counter to what may currently reign as vogue.

"Pathfinders" will function in the role of leaders and teachers. These persons will engage in direct action. They have chosen to live the mantra, "willing to go the distance to make a difference." That difference shall manifest as Nation Building. Nationhood will never come into existence, if haphazardly approached. The tactic must appear systemic in nature. Spelled out clearly and succinctly, the non-negotiables will present a detailed memorandum of understanding. Nation Building shall proffer an alternative to the symmetrical acts of oppression, withdrawal from the current system as a necessity. In order for those, who have been excluded by this coeval system to have an opportunity of meaningful and positive productivity, an egress has become an essential next step. Nation Building's clarion call will not ask for small incremental withdrawal from the present norms of contemporary society, but will command a vertex leap to advance the people. Primarily, the imperfect people and the impoverished people no longer have any value to the current system. Nation Building will hold a much higher mantle than a catharsis. Nation Building will never have confinement as solely a theory. Nation Building will not rest as a hypothesis, plying to bring a complex ideology to consciousness. Nation Building will never seek for a moment of expression only to end in a decimated experience and eliminated as a non-action philosophy. Nation Building will command an action that shall produce a channel for maximum individual and collective group production, all for the maximum good of the populace.

Bibliography:

NATION BUILDING: VOLUME I, Portrait of a Movement (the Transition to Nation Building): Apostle Mark Carven Olds, 2008.

NATION BUILDING: VOLUME II, The Pillars (Theology and Infrastructure): Apostle Mark Carven Olds, 2008.

NATION BUILDING: VOLUME IV, The Pathway – The Collage: Apostle Mark carven Olds, 2008.

INIC Invitation:

The Immanuel Nation In Christ (INIC) will welcome all into a classless society, but none into a faithless society. The INIC will extend an invitation to all, who wish to exit the current system and have the willpower to leave behind the ways of the old methods. The egress will represent more than a change of address or a move to a new place. This egress will convey a move away from the practice of injustice, in-equality, and repressive ideology. All persons, who shall desire to live covenant, will find the encouragement to partake of this undertaking. Individuals must have a preparation experience in their souls to walk by faith into a theocratic, interdependent, and peaceful society. This classless society will welcome:

Imperfect people[1] *– persons who have received labels from the dominant society which discredit or prohibit participation; coded or labeled less than arbitrary standard set by society; convicted criminal; or arrested on a criminal charge; or other less than model measures of society.*

Impoverished people[2] *– the less fortunate in terms of financial possessions; those whose income is below the poverty level; limited economic opportunity.*

Justice seekers[3] *– persons who look for ways and means to practice fairness and righteousness both as individuals and as a society.*

Progressive individuals[4] *– people who are politically astute; cognizant of the need for change which bring about solutions; persons willing to work for the advancement of all people in society.*

<u>Skilled laborers</u>[5] — *individuals with multiple experiences in various faucets of life; experienced in ministry, profession, or vocation; tradesmen or diplomats.*

The INIC Invitation shall call out to born-again Believers, covenant living practitioners, and all who have committed to the greater good of the total populace.

Notes:

[1,2,3,4,5]Nation Building: Volume IV, The Pathway – The Collage

INIC Declaration of Interdependence:

The Immanuel Nation In Christ will call for covenant living practitioners, who shall rely on a Covenant-Keeping God to raise up a nation that will practice righteousness and justice. The INIC shall emerge as a classless society that will extend an opportunity for each individual to obtain access to the resources that will empower them to reach their full potential both naturally and spiritually. No good thing will be withheld from those who will walk uprightly. The INIC shall make known its position officially, formally, and explicitly.

The goal of the INIC will always resound to assemble in unity a people, who shall live to perform reciprocity through trusting, sharing, and relying upon one another. This collective effort will produce a quality state of living. Such a collective equality view of life will have been influenced and determined by a people who will measure the greater good of the populace, rather than the promotion of an individual achievement. The INIC shall exhibit the interdependence of its citizenry upon one another. When one citizen hurts, all the citizenry will hurt. When one citizen rejoices, and the citizenry shall rejoice. When the populace has a quality life existence, then the INIC will exist as a quality nation that shall administer justice for all.

Bases upon the covenants of the Father, the teachings of Jesus, and the Holy Spirit's indwelling Believers, interdependence has been Divinely mandated. The Father has made His children[1] equal by His grace through faith.[2] His children have been declared heirs and joint-heirs with

Jesus. Christ would further teach that we should love our neighbors as ourselves. By doing so, others would become cognizant that have become disciples by our love for one another.[3] The Holy Spirit has enabled us to be to fulfill this non-grievous command. Love has been shed abroad in our hearts by the Holy Spirit.[4]The INIC Declaration of Interdependence will produce a reality destined for belief because of the works,[5] its fruit, as well as the results of obedience as an integral part of covenant living.

Notes:

[1]Romans 8:14 KJV

[2]Ephesians 2:8 NASB

[3]John 13:34-35 NIV

[4]Romans 5:5 KJV

[5]John 14:11 KJV

INIC Preamble to the Constitution:

You shall love your neighbor as yourself.[1] If there is a poor man with you, one of your brothers, in any of your towns in your land which the Lord your God is giving you, you shall not harden your heart, nor close your hand from your brother; but you shall freely open your hand to him, and shall generously lend him sufficient for his need in whatever he lacks.[2] For God so loved the world that He gave His one and only Son, that whoever believes in Him shall not perish but have eternal life.[3] Now faith is the substance of things hoped for, the evidence of things not seen.[4] But without faith it is impossible to please and be satisfactory to Him. For whoever would come near to God must [necessarily] believe that God exists and that He is the rewarder of those who earnestly and diligently seek Him [out].[5] He has told you, O man, what is good; And what does the Lord require of you but to do justice, to love kindness, And to walk humbly with your God.[6] I will make a covenant of peace with them; it will be an everlasting covenant. I will establish them and increase their numbers, and I will put my sanctuary among them forever. My dwelling place will be with them; I will be their God, and they will be my people.[7]

Notes:

[1]Matthew 19:19b NASB – Unconditional love.

[2]Deuteronomy 15:7-8 NASB – Openhanded care of one another.

[3]John 3:16 NIV – Evangelism – rebirth first requirement of INIC citizenship.

[4]Hebrews 11:1 KJV – Faith to seek God diligently.

[5]Hebrews 11:6 AMPLIFIED – God is a rewarder.

[6]Micah 6:8 NASB – Administer justice, love mercy, walk humbly before God.

[7]Ezkiel 37_26-27 NIV – Everlasting Covenant of Peace.

INIC Constitution:

I. You shall have no other gods before Me.[1]

II. You shall not make yourself any graven image [to worship it] or any likeness of anything that is in the heavens above, or that is in the earth beneath, or that is in the water under the earth.[2]

III. You shall not take the name of the Lord your God in vain.[3]

IV. Remember the Sabbath day, to keep it holy[4]

V. Honor your father and your mother, that your days may be prolonged in the land which the Lord your God gives you.[5]

VI. You shall not murder.[6]

VII. You shall not commit adultery.[7]

VIII. You shall not steal.[8]

IX. You shall not give false testimony against your neighbor.[9]

X. You shall not covet your neighbor's house. You shall not covet your neighbor's wife, or his manservant or maidservant, his ox or donkey, or anything that belongs to your neighbor.[10]

NOTES:

[1]Exodus 20:3 NASB

[2]Exodus 20:4 AMPLIFIED

[3]Exodus 20:7a NASB

[4]Exodus 20:8 NASB

[5]Exodus 20:12 NASB

[6]Exodus 20:13 NASB

[7]Exodus 20:14 NASB

[8]Exodus 20:15 NASB

[9]Exodus 20:16 NIV

[10]Exodus 20:17 NIV

INIC Constitutional Amendments:

I. The community is to have the same rules for you and for the alien living among you; this is a lasting ordinance for the generations to come. You and the alien shall be the same before the Lord.[1]

II. "The time is coming," declares the Lord, "when I will make a new covenant with the house of Israel and with the house of Judah. It will not be like the covenant I made with their forefathers when I took them by the hand to lead them out of Egypt, because they broke my covenant, though I was a husband to them," declares the Lord." This is the covenant I will make with the house of Israel after that time," declares the Lord. "I will put my law in their minds and write it on their hearts. I will be their God, and they will be my people. No longer will a man teach his neighbor, or a man his brother, saying, 'Know the Lord,' because they will all know me, from the least of them to the greatest," declares the Lord. "For I will forgive their wickedness and will remember their sins no more."[2]

III. Love is patient, love is kind. It does not envy, it does not boast, it is not proud. It is not rude, it is not self-seeking, it is not easily angered, it keeps no record of wrongs. Love does not delight in evil but rejoices with the truth. It always protects, always trusts, always hopes, always perseveres. Love never fails.[3]

IV. For with God nothing is ever impossible and no word from God shall be without power or impossible of fulfillment.[4]

V. A new commandment I give to you, that you love one another, even as I have loved you, that you also love one another.[5]

Notes:

[1]Numbers 15:15 NIV

[2]Jeremiah 31:31-33 NIV

[3]1 Corinthians 13:4-8a NIV

[4]Luke 1:37 AMPLIFIED

[5]John 13:34 NASB

INIC Assurance of Blessings – Bill of Promises

I. Blessed are the poor in spirit: for theirs is the kingdom of heaven.[1]

II. Blessed are they that mourn: for they shall be comforted.[2]

III. Blessed are the meek: for they shall inherit the earth.[3]

IV. Blessed are they which do hunger and thirst after righteousness: for they shall be filled.[4]

V. Blessed are the merciful: for they shall obtain mercy.[5]

VI. Blessed are the pure in heart: for they shall see God.[6]

VII. Blessed are the peacemakers: for they shall be called the children of God.[7]

VIII. Blessed are they which are persecuted for righteousness' sake: for theirs is the kingdom of heaven.[8]

IX. Blessed are you when people insult you and persecute you, and falsely say all kinds of evil against you because of Me.[9]

Notes:

[1]Matthew 5:3 KJV

[2]Matthew 5:4 KJV

[3]Matthew 5:5 KJV

[4]Matthew 5:6 KJV

[5]Matthew 5:7 KJV

[6]Matthew 5:8 KJV

[7]Matthew 5:9 KJV

[8]Matthew 5:10 KJV

[9]Matthew 5:11 NASB

INIC Anthem:

The Immanuel Nation In Christ's Anthem (the Anthem) will construct an arrangement in artistic splendor that will arrive as a sacred composition, a song, as well as a hymn of praise and gladness. Adoration and joy, passion and fulfillment shall echo a sensitivity of accomplishment as each note will float melodiously from heart to heart and breast to breast.

The Anthem for the imperfect people and the impoverished people shall extend beyond guilt or innocence, poverty or wealth. God alone can justify or make provisions. The Anthem cannot categorize itself as too bluesy, draining the emotions and pulling the spirit into depression. It cannot on an overly festive mood, launching a false sense of euphoria. The Anthem will have to release an ability to summon forgiveness and a capability to embrace a new life of expectation and maximum potential realization.

Mourning time has passed. The Anthem must filter the spirit as a message of hope. It must have the power to comfort all who shall mourn even as nation time has arrived. The oil of gladness has manifested through Nation Building.

The Anthem shall patiently await the time of its written advent. It must contain the rhythm and energy of Whitehead and McFadden's, "Ain't No Stopping Us Now." But, it must also contain the reverence and sacredness of James Weldon Johnson's, "Lift Every Voice And Sing."

Listeners to the Anthem must hear words that were delivered by Frederick Douglas, Harriet Tubman, Robert Kennedy, and Martin Luther King, Jr., while the vocals of

Aretha Franklin, Mavis Staples, Carole King, James Taylor, Otis Redding, and Mahalia Jackson shall translate the utterances from mind to spirit.

The author (or authors) shall display musical genius, only God can anoint and inspire the composer for this assignment. The pen of the ready writer may exist as a wordsmith alike William "Smokey" Robinson, or the psalmist may have the inspiration from the Holy Spirit in the manner of a Thomas Dorsey.

The music must move the feet to take on the nimbleness of Bill "Bojangles" Robinson, or the graceful finesse of that was illustrated in Sammy Davis, Jr. Yet, the composition must embrace the spirit of an unnamed mother dancing in the Holy Ghost before an awesome God at a small Sanctified and Holiness Church. The background music must also capture the backstory accompanied with the sounds of stomping feet, a tambourine, and snare drum providing both a cadence and the rhythm.

Perhaps, the Anthem's author may have to wait until the Immanuel Nation In Christ has been fully formed.

Perhaps, the words and melody will only mesh the teaching of Nation Building.

Perhaps, the Anthem will serve as a tool to help the Immanuel Nation In Christ expand its territory and mission. In such an application or scenario, the Anthem's emergence should not face delay.

Perhaps, the Anthem's author has not yet been conceived. The parents may meet over dialogue surrounding Nation Building.

The individual, who shall pen the Anthem, may not have yet converted to Christianity or even embraced Nation Building. In such an experience, evangelism, education, and enactment should not face delay.

The Anthem? Everyone will know it when they hear, feel, and embrace the message of the Immanuel Nation In Christ, flowing throughout their very being with the passionate fire of the Holy Ghost.

The Anthem? The melody will soar with the grace, flair, confidence, enthusiasm, and uniqueness of Michael Jordan slashing and leaping for an artistic basket, while the rhythmic beat will demonstrate the power, raw energy, commitment, courage, and resilience of George Foreman marching to regain the heavyweight championship.

The Anthem? A single musical rendition may not possess or have the capacity capable of capturing the spirit and faith of nation. It may require a compilation or an extensive volume of sacred music; only then, may the music emerge to tell the story of Nation Building.

INIC Flag:

The Immanuel Nation In Christ's Flag (the Flag) shall beckon to its designer to come forth with a spirit of justice. The artistic rendering must shoulder an identification with equality, love, and righteousness. The Flag must reign as more than symbolic. Upon making visual contact, one must rise in the spirit to feel that they have been wrapped in the message of the Immanuel Nation In Christ.

The virtues that shall have representation by the Flag must attract individuals to Nation Building. The Flag should strike a musical cord within the hearts of those who will see it waving by the distant winds. Those, who will stand close enough to hear the flapping sounds, should have a recollection of past victories and future struggles to overcome. The Flag should ignite a flame that will illumine an identity with the Immanuel Nation In Christ.

Upon viewing the Flag, the imperfect people and the impoverished people should envision an end to disenfranchisement and exclusion from the current system, while the Flag shall represent restoration, opportunity, inclusion, and healing. The skilled laborers, progressive individuals, and justice seekers shall perceive a classless society.

The Immanuel Nation In Christ's Flag should never foster serve as simply a symbolic flag freedom, but the Flag should represent an egress from the world system and entrance into God's kingdom.

INIC Seal

The Immanuel Nation In Christ's Seal (the Seal) will be affixed to official documents to determine irrevocably a contractual validation. In addition to satiating legal requirements, the Seal shall guarantee the will and approval of a covenant living people. Because the Seal will represent the people, it shall exceed the symbolism of a bureaucratic stamp. The Immanuel Nation In Christ's Seal should never appear on a document or any cause irresponsibly. The Seal shall invoke the trustworthiness of a nation. The Immanuel Nation In Christ's Seal will proclaim the obligatory statements pledged will prove authenticate.

The design, the artistic rendition will await the disciple on Nation Building to come forth. The Seal will represent one of the areas that has remained incomplete, because the revelation and the designer have not yet merged.

The Baedeker to Nationhood

Authored by: Mark Carven Olds, MNO

List Price: **$24.95   6" x 9"**
Black & White on White Paper   278 pages
ISBN-13: 978-1517586560 (CreateSpace-Assigned)
ISBN-10: 1517586569
BISAC: Political Science / Political Ideologies / Democracy
The conundrum that will surround Nation Building can be found in the de-mystification of the programmatic intent.
ISBN-10: 1517586569
BISAC: Political Science / Political Ideologies / Democracy
The conundrum that will surround Nation Building can be found in the de-mystification of the programmatic intent.
Nation Building will not threaten the people by coercion or the government with violence. Nation Building will sustain an ostracized people with hope and shall invoke a number of tangible economic endeavors as a methodology to lessen their

dependence upon the existing system. Nationhood will help eliminate its citizenry from the welfare rolls, public housing subsidies, entitlement programs, and healthcare supplements. In addition, nationhood status will significantly help reduce the number of individuals on probation, parole, and confined in penal colonies. At the same time, nationhood will create entrepreneurial opportunities, build businesses, provide jobs, and reduce school dropout rates. Nationhood will also provide the illustration of covenant living through a Theocratic Interdependent Peaceful Society (T.I.P.S.). The fast pace of everyday life can often remove the analytical process that may reduce the nationhood emergence to many as a complicated riddle or an impossible feat to produce. When the analysis has been applied to Nation Building as if to a job related initiative, personal involvement will then cause the view of systemic change to take on a more proportional advancement. In other words, it can be seen in smaller steps that will lead to a massive undertaken. However, the colossal venture of Nation Building will never seem doable to a people who have been cemented to only function in the current system.

CreateSpace eStore: https://www.createspace.com/5770775

Also Available: Amazon.com * Amazon Europe * Kindle * Bookstores and Online Retailers

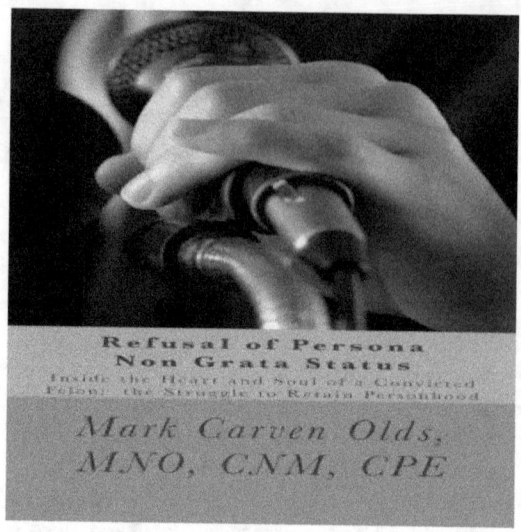

Project Summary

Refusal of Persona Non Grata Status:
Inside the Heart and Soul of a Convicted Felon:
the Struggle to Retain

Personhood
Authored by: Mr. Mark Carven Olds, MNO

List Price: **$14.95**
6" x 9" (15.24 x 22.86 cm)
Black & White on White paper 66 pages
ISBN-13: 978-1512209198 (CreateSpace-Assigned)
ISBN-10: 1512209198 BISAC: Self-Help / Motivational &
Inspirational
"Refusal of Persona Non Grata Status. Inside the Heart and Soul of a
Convicted
Felon: The Struggle to Retain Personhood"

      This volume will take you inside not merely a physical
prison, but the spiritual battle to stay focused as a valued human
being. This work captures a personal experience to remain a
person and not become a number. In this exertion, I reflect on the
twelve stages of spiritual, physical, mental, and emotional warfare
that I encountered daily. These skirmishes are not written in any
manual, but they are real in the heart and soul of anyone who has

been incarcerated. So many of those incarcerated become the victim of failure to the spiritual and psychological warfare that greets an individual upon the loss of freedom.

Unbroken Anguish, Relentless Battles, Shaping Destiny or Impacting History, as well as Humility and Wisdom are among the twelve stages of warfare that must be fought and won in order to retain personhood. The Refusal of Persona Non Grata Status represents a vital key that will unlock the door of hope for a positive future.

The Refusal of Persona Non Grata Status assures the individual that in spite of the opposing odds, giving up and succumbing to failure or a lower class designation is not an option, nor an alternative.

Allow me to interject, all prisons are not constructed with concrete and steel. There are many emotional, financial, mental, and spiritual prisons that have higher numerical populations than all the global criminal justice systems combined. In this exertion, the foundation has been lain to help anyone through any dilemma that would threaten their personhood. This is a clarion call to anyone who may have felt victimized or demeaned in character. The Refusal of Persona Non Grata Status will help you to reach a victorious plateau over the twelve battle stages of spiritual warfare that seek to destroy your personhood.

CreateSpace eStore: https://www.createspace.com/5499596
ALSO AVAILABLE: Amazon.com * Amazon Europe * Kindle
* Bookstores and Online Retailers

Mark Carven Olds has evolved as a sage voice of leadership in the African-

American community and beyond. His emergence and resurgence has been spurred by a unique fusion of multifaceted life experiences. He has procured a viable presence in the academic, faith, and political environs. He has earned a Master of Nonprofit Organizations degree from Case Western Reserve University, Cleveland, Ohio. He has also done post graduate studies at Case's History Department. He has also done doctoral studies at the Union Institute & University in

Interdisciplinary Studies with a Specialization in Public Policy/Health, Cincinnati, Ohio. He has always and will continue to strive for fresh plateaus that may enhance the quality of life for all humanity.

Mark Carven Olds has founded a number of nonprofit organizations that have had local and national impact. Two of his latest endeavors, the Midwest Minority Think Tank for Public Policy, Leadership, and Service, LLC. and the Midwest Minority Think Tank Foundation, LLC., were launched to serve the people in whatever realm that a conundrum may arise.

CONTACT DATA:

Blog: www.themidwestthinktank.com

Web Site: www.midwestminoritythinktank.com
Justice, Liberation & Salvation Youtube Channel:

https://www.youtube.com/channel/UCQF4Tr0bYyJ9s8 8uskvRCHA

YouTube: Mark Carven Olds

Facebook: www.facebook.com/MarkCOlds

Twitter: https://twitter.com/midwestminority

Email: markcarvenolds@midwestminoritythinktank.com

Or   mcolds49@gmail.com

Cell: 216.389.4340

Project Summary

A Complex Issue: **(A Succinct Apothegmatic of Nation Building)**
Authored by Mr. Mark Carven Olds

List Price: **$24.95 6" x 9"** (15.24 x 22.86 cm) Black & White on

White paper 182 pages
ISBN-13: 978-1518754555 (CreateSpace-Assigned)
ISBN-10: 1518754554
BISAC: Political Science / Political Ideologies / General

Nationhood shall appear as a conundrum to the coeval elements of power; thus, evoking an automatic propaganda campaign to label the endeavor as disingenuous. Nation Building will garner the attention of those designated to lower class status. The process shall call for an egression from the prevalent system. A noncompliant attitude toward acceptance of an inferior position will signal the need for both economic and social recalibration. By an ongoing disparity practice of the wealth and resources of the world, nationhood status for the imperfect people and the impoverished people will present a predicament or quandary to the commerce arena as currently in universal practice. Up to this point, the imperfect people and the impoverished people have failed to control any industry domestically or globally. However, the practice of collective economics by them can rearrange the methods that current industries exercise in the manner that they conduct commerce with the less fortunate.

Nation Building will reveal itself as a riddle, awaiting to be resolved by both the recipients of nationhood status and those who will vehemently oppose its mission. When the Doctrine of Nation Building has been fully exposed to the multitudes who have been confined in the valley of decision, "the powers that be" and "the people in the valley" will seek a more transparent resolution. "The powers that be" will recognize a people have arrived at a strength that will demand change. "The people (who will most likely enter the citizenry of a new nation)" shall finally realize the capacity of their potential to make a significant change work. The raising of a new nation will alter the existing order and those who have been subject to its existing edicts. A venture that will order the construct of power re-configuration shall command attention far beyond a small political caucus. The origin of an initiative that shall depict

"transcending values" will refuse corner isolation, nor can the subject matter be relegated to a vacuum status.

Whatever the insightful basis or the centripetal reflective of a new concept, the opposition shall swell and escalate. The dissemination of an antipodal message will accelerate with energy. In fact, the opposition will help propel the message with avid communication across the landscape. The key for the Nation Builder will always remain to keep tight control of the message. The very pronouncement of nationhood shall issue an invitation for persecution. Nation Builders must understand the role of designated leaders and gatekeepers. They have a dual task to undermine the move toward nationhood, while spewing the venomous speech of the opposition. In spite of these anticipatory opposition factors, Nation Builders have no option other than to press forward with the agenda of Nation Building.

CreateSpace eStore: https://www.createspace.com/5820639

List Price: **$24.95**
6" x 9" (15.24 x 22.86 cm) Black & White on White Paper - 124 pages
ISBN-13: **978-1523431410** (CreateSpace-Assigned)
ISBN-10: **1523431415** BISAC: **History / Historiography**

A movement should always be greater than its leader. "A Portrait of a Movement" will illustrate the multiple factors which shall be at work both pro and con. Nation Building can only be achieved by a number of committed people.

This volume will shed light on "the why" people "do or do not" embrace change. Among the most significant aspects of this work will be the recognition of the timing of God.

Such recognition will give or deny success to a movement. "I declared the former things long ago and they went forth from my mouth, and I proclaimed them. Suddenly I acted, and they came to pass." (Isaiah 48:3 NASB) It was further proclaimed by the prophet

Isaiah, "Even from eternity I am He, and there is none who can deliver out of my hand;
I   act   and   who   can   reverse it?"   (Isaiah 43:13   NASB) The attrition of developments in life will come mostly as unforeseeable. They shall come to test our endurance, faith, and commitment. Especially tested will be our vows to solve problems related to community which may bring about societal change. Personally, it has become excruciatingly painful to think of having lived for decades and not contributing to the positive change for people who have suffered under oppression and injustice. Of all the experiences that I have undergone, my living will have been in vain – If conditions have worsen at my demise than they were at my birth. This should not be interpreted in some morbid sense, nor should it be looked upon as delusional thinking. I will simply possess great faith. I cannot accept less than the unlimited potential that has always resided within me.

CreateSpace eStore: https://www.createspace.com/6002652

Nation Building: Volume II - The Pillars: (Theology and Infrastructure)

Authored by Mr. Mark Carven Olds

List Price: **$24.95   6" x 9"** (15.24 x 22.86 cm)   Black & White on White paper   104 pages

ISBN-13: 978-1530513598 (CreateSpace-Assigned)
ISBN-10: 1530513596
BISAC: Political Science / Political Process / Leadership

Divine essence shall make it imperative that the Immanuel Nation In Christ (INIC) will arise now. Unexplainable events shall always occur in human history to point humanity to the Creator. Imperfect people and impoverished people will have to assume the role of "Pathfinders." No other options shall avail them to find their Divine destiny. Equal status can only mean being a nation the same as others. Ostracism has made quality an impossibility in the current system. Rather than accept a life as a second class citizen, Nation Building shall provide equality, respect, and opportunity.

First, nation has to be defined. Webster has put forth the following definition: A stable, historically developed of people with a territory, economic life, distinctive culture, and language in common. The following will detail an examination of the six points within the definition of nation.

It would be ludicrous to expect all people to respond affirmatively to Nation Building. Affirmation shall come from those who have ears to hear the voice of the Spirit. Theocracy will never alter a Divine Plan based on democracy. God shall speak that which does not exist into being. His omniscience will appoint the time existing systems and reigning powers shall witness a new standard of moral excellence and consecrated holiness.

The injustices that have been rehearsed against the imperfect people and the impoverished people will rest at the heart of the Immanuel Nation In Christ (INIC) and Nation Building. God will raise up the INIC to show His mercy and power on behalf of the oppressed. The Father shall exhibit His faithfulness as a God of Justice. Nation Building shall arise as God will triumph over wickedness and the abuse of the less fortunate. The Jewish nation had arisen as God would use them to execute judgment on the occupiers of Palestine. Whenever the wicked prevail over the meek, God will intervene. He shall plant a people to become His witness. The imperfect people and the impoverished people of this era will be used by God to demonstrate His love and compassion. By raising up a nation in this contemporary age, God will do so without preference or bias. He shall do so by choosing the weak or the least enviable to show His great and authentic power.

The emergence of the Immanuel Nation in Christ (INIC) will awaken people who have been trapped in poverty and disenfranchised from the current political system. God has not reclined un-attentively to human activity. He has not chosen a heavenly view to keep vigil as the world affairs unfold. His instructions shall provide victorious strategies over the opposition's most brilliant designs of oppression.

The exertion shall raise the consciousness of the imperfect people, impoverished people, progressive individuals, and justice seekers to the level of Nation Building. The compulsory measures toward Nation Building will be explored in this volume. Within the content of this material, the imperfect people and impoverished people shall receive the resolution and determination to cherish Nation Building. The progressive individuals and justice seekers will find the spiritual, intellectual, and theoretical mix to invoke Nation Building.

CreateSpace eStore: https://www.createspace.com/6135390